10-31-85

Cliff & Laura — Happy Halloween!

It would be fun to share some time with good friends like you in this beautiful state someday! Let's do it!

Love,
Amy & Bruno

CALIF

PREFACE

LOS ANGELES

SAN FRANCISCO

THE COAST

DESERTS

MOUNTAINS

Published by Gallery Books
A Division of W H Smith Publishers Inc.
112 Madison Avenue
New York, New York 10016

Produced by
Bison Books Corp.
17 Sherwood Place
Greenwich, CT 06830

ISBN 0-8317-1151-5

Printed in Hong Kong
1 2 3 4 5 6 7 8 9 10

ORNIA

PHOTOGRAPHY	MARCELLO BERTINETTI ANGELA WHITE BERTINETTI
TEXT	VALERIA MANFERTO DE FABIANIS
DESIGN	CARLO DE FABIANIS

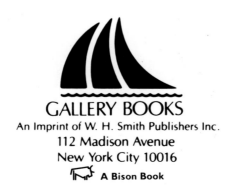

GALLERY BOOKS
An Imprint of W. H. Smith Publishers Inc.
112 Madison Avenue
New York City 10016
A Bison Book

The authors gratefully acknowledge the
help of: Gianna Manferto, Giorgio
Tacchini, The Bank of America and Italy,
Trans World Airlines, the Fairmont Hotel
of San Francisco.

Photographs on pages 65, 71, 82 and 87
are by Carlo and Valeria De Fabianis.
Photograph on pages 94-5 is by Ugo
Monetti.

*3-6 One of the most magnificent parts of the
California coast is Big Sur which stretches
from Carmel to San Luis Obispo. Many
species of sea birds and rare wildlife can be
found among the rugged cliffs and secluded
beaches.*

Preface

After World War II, California underwent incredible development in the fields of commerce and industry. California cities began to spread out beyond their earlier limits, becoming the megalopolises they are today, characterized by huge mobile populations, chaotic and feverish traffic and frenzied working patterns.

This rapid development also created serious social troubles, culminating during the sixties in student protests and unrest among the ethnic minorities. Nevertheless, the Golden State has continued its endless economic ascent, determined in part by the lucky union of modern industry to high quality technology. Actually California is the most flourishing state in the Union. If it were an independent country it would be one of the most powerful industrial nations in the world.

The most striking and obvious example of this social and economic progress is the so-called Silicon Valley. Ten years ago this area, which is found only a few miles outside San Francisco, between Palo Alto and San Jose, was nothing more than a series of vineyards, orchards and truck farms; today it is a world center of the micro-electronic industry with more than a thousand companies and a working population of 225,000.

California not only goes with the times, in many aspects it runs ahead, being by its own nature a land always looking to the future. One of the reasons for this is education. California has one of the highest educational levels per capita in the United States. Over 20 percent of the population has a university education, and this percentage is bound to increase. A sound scholastic preparation and high technology seem to be the key to California's success and achievements in both individual and national fields. It can be said that California is experiencing another gold rush. While most other countries are suffering through serious economic crises, California is leading the United States in an incredible growth, establishing itself once more as the land of great achievements.

The natural resources, the climate, the geographic position and the pioneer nature of the population are the main elements of the winning and successful character of the Golden State, which today still represents and embodies the American Dream. Glory, fame and wealth seem to be within everyone's reach. Everything seems possible, and even the impossible can be achieved with success. Trust and a certain optimism seem to be present everywhere. Obviously such hopes and dreams do not always come true, often reality intrudes, especially in the big cities, such as Los Angeles or Sacramento. The reality of hard work can be found everywhere, but in California everybody seems to have the opportunity to cultivate some dreams. The obvious charm of California may be due in part to this attitude, but there is also the incredible variety of landscape not easily equalled elsewhere. Californians seem to respect their country deeply, and, outside the cities and industrial areas, become involved seriously in preserving this beauty, from the arid peace of the deserts and the majesty of the great forests, to the mountain wilderness, the green fertility of the valleys and the extraordinary beauty of the Pacific Coast. This attitude is found in young and old alike. I once had the opportunity to hear a group of young people singing beside a campfire in one of the great national parks, and through their voices felt the heroes of America's past come to life again, with all the dreams and aspirations that have created the basis of American life today.

American history is short, but reminders of the past can be found throughout the state, from the parched land of Death Valley to the old logging camps of the Northern forests. The daylight effect on the sand of the desert gives it the appearance of a lunar landscape, strange and beautiful, the work of nature, not man. Equally the violence of the ocean waves on the coast where the mists of early spring combine with the spume of waves on Big Sur to mask the landscape, inspires mystical feelings for the power of nature.

California can be defined therefore as a place of great emotions, in line with the strength of the landscape and the power of the cities. Californians live on these strong feelings and emotions, and out of their common quest to succeed create something unique.

More than any other state, California embodies the principles and values which, supported by an unshakeable will, have given the United States the difficult role of the leading nation in the world. On the tanned faces of her citizens you can easily trace the justified satisfaction of being part of a great country and in contributing day after day to that greatness through development and continuous social and economic progress.

The American Dream is more alive in California than anywhere else.

Valeria Manferto De Fabianis

Los Angeles

In the middle of the eighteenth century, a Spanish military expedition arrived at the point of land in the Mexican province of California where the city of Los Angeles now lies. After a journey through the arid mountains and deserts, the members of the expedition were amazed by the fertility and beauty that surrounded them. Trees were thriving, and the climate seemed favorable to settlement. Beginning as the Mission San Gabriel at Nuestra Señora de Los Angeles de Porcuincula, built by the Franciscan Father Junipero Serra, a settlement grew up to provide food for the garrisons at San Diego and Santa Barbara. With the help of the missionaries, the Shoshone tribe cooperated with the colonists, mingling with the Spanish population.

Economic and social development followed, and while the city was still governed by the newly independent Mexico, economically there were strong ties to the United States. At the outbreak of the Mexican War in 1846, California declared itself a republic, and was admitted to statehood in 1850.

The passage of California from territory to State, and the discovery of gold near Sacramento, had been the first steps in the radical change of Los Angeles from a border village to a modern city. Several ethnic invasions followed the Spanish one attracted by the mirage of easy riches. The full integration of these groups is not yet complete, and that path has been highlighted by periods of extreme violence. Rapid growth and the discovery of oil have also played a part in this development. By the 1920s Los Angeles was the largest city in the world by area, and it kept growing as the movie industry and various aspects of agriculture established themselves in the surrounding area. Technological advances in the 1950s brought increased economic development as well as the first upheavels of the youth movement.

Today Los Angeles is one of the most important cities in the United States, still looking towards the future. Its dimensions are vast, and include landscapes that differ from one another completely: long and wide beaches, deserts, mountains and cultivated hills.

Apart from the downtown skyscrapers, the city has grown out, not up, and is characterized by a huge expanse of low houses and an unbelievable number of swimming pools.

Los Angeles more than any other American city embodies the myth of success. Dreams of fame, glory and wealth seem more likely to come true, and nowhere is this feeling more evident than in Hollywood, still synonymous with glamour and power. Everything there seems to have different dimensions and work by different rules.

The people of Los Angeles seem equally different: carefree, easy-going, suntanned and a little bit showy, they can be distinctly businesslike and hardworking despite casual appearances. This perhaps is the true image of Los Angeles: the easy and carefree manner disguising the hard logic of business and economic interest.

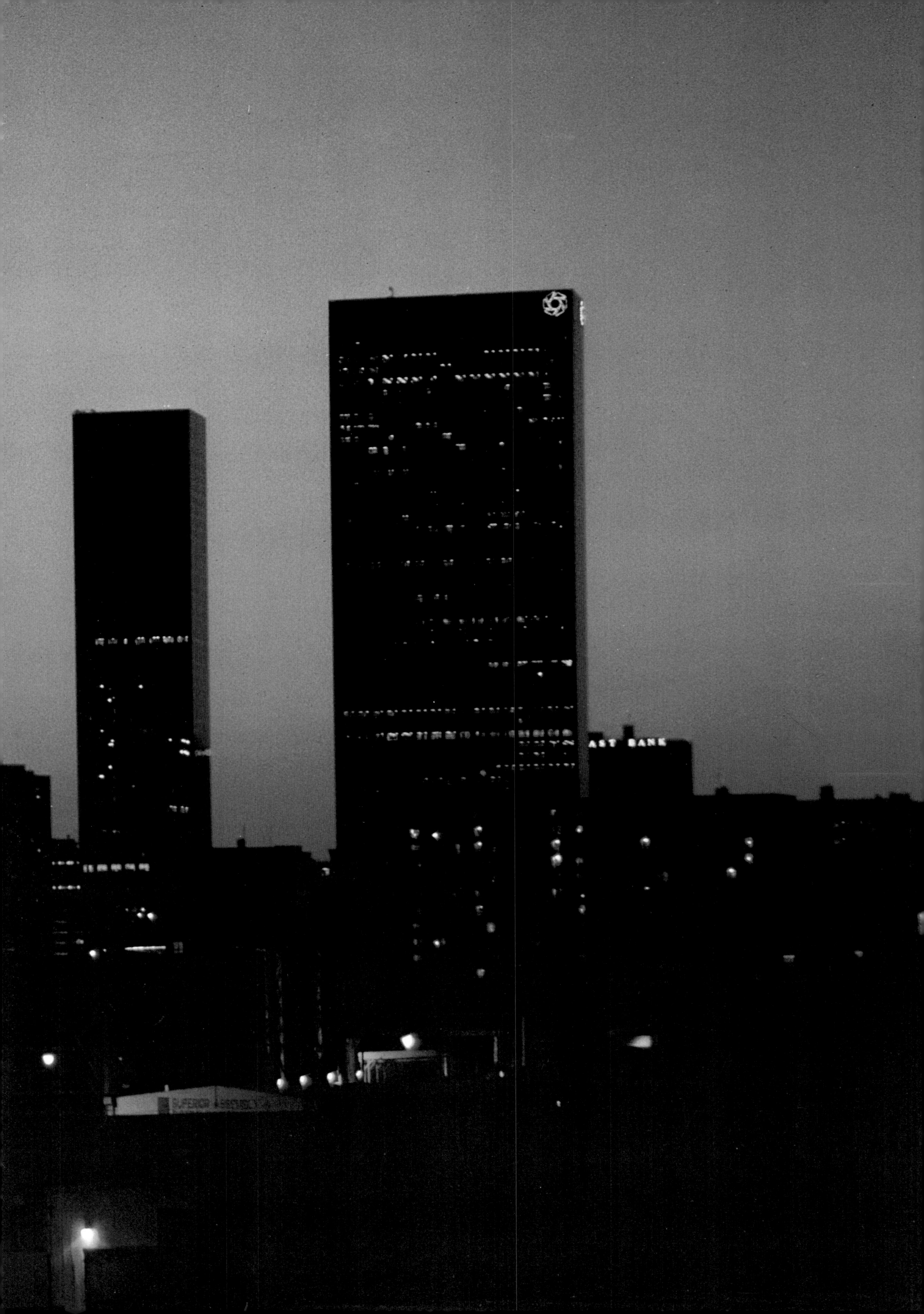
AST BANK
SUPERIOR

14 Covering an area of 464 square miles, Greater Los Angeles includes many small cities and towns as well as the modern skyscrapers of downtown Los Angeles.

15 A sunset view of the Bonaventure Hotel which was designed by architect John Portman. The glass exterior elevator brings visitors up to the rooftop terrace where they can enjoy an incomparable view of the city.

16-18 The unique skyline of Los Angeles is silhouetted against a sunset sky intensified by the smog which occasionally descends upon the city.

19 Modern sculpture such as the work seen here at the Atlantic Ridgefield Plaza is displayed throughout the city.

20-21 Within the commercial center of the city can be found the highest skyscrapers which include a number of important architectural works.

22-23 An extraordinary view of the skyscrapers surrounding the Security Pacific Plaza seen through the frame of a modern freestanding sculpture.

24-25 The freeways of Los Angeles surround the city and are used by over five million cars each day.

26 The circular towers of the Bonaventure Hotel reflected in a skyscraper window. The Bonaventure includes five floors of select shops and a revolving lounge.

27 Somber skyscrapers stand out against the clear Los Angeles sky.

28-29 *A glorious sunset gilds the sky on a quiet street that climbs one of many hills of Los Angeles.*

30 *The popular beach at Venice, close to Santa Monica, is almost three miles long, and a favorite spot for weekend roller skaters and bicyclists.*

31 The yacht basin at Marina del Ray, the largest along the Pacific Coast, has moorings for over 10,000 pleasure boats.

32-33 The amenities of Santa Monica State Beach, including surfing, volleyball, bike paths and fishing off the famous pier, make it one of the most popular in the area.

34-35 Dodger Stadium, the home of Los Angeles' famous baseball team, can seat over 56,000 fans and, unlike many stadiums, still boasts a grass surface.

36-37 *The population of Los Angeles is made up of many different ethnic groups, but the Blacks and the Mexicans seem to predominate.*

38 *Rodeo Drive, in Beverly Hills, is one of the most elegant and expensive shopping areas in Los Angeles.*

39 Beverly Hills, where many movie stars and millionaires built extravagant houses, lies northwest of Los Angeles, close to the San Gabriel Range and not far away from Hollywood.

40 *The extraordinary facade of Frederick's, the world famous purveyor of lingerie, is typical of the unusual buildings found in Hollywood.*

41 Sunset Boulevard, well-known as the title
of a great Gloria Swanson movie, is still the
center of Los Angeles night life.

42 John Travolta, among other stars, attend-
ing a film premiere at Graumann's Chinese
Theater. Since 1927 Graumann's has been
a name synonymous with the glamour of
Hollywood.

43 Elegance and sophistication are still the
hallmarks of the Hollywood star.

San Francisco

In 1906, the city of San Francisco was almost leveled by the twin disasters of earthquake and fire. For months, thousands of people camped out in tents, running businesses, raising their families and rebuilding the city as they had planned before those last flames were extinguished.

Situated in a most favorable natural site, San Francisco is without doubt one of the most charming and beloved of all American cities. Unlike many other modern cities, San Francisco doesn't allow the anxiety of most industrial cities to prevail. Everywhere there is a sense of happy relaxation, of harmony and a natural way of living.

It is not easy to identify and describe the individual elements which make up the special charm of this city. Maybe it is the streets, which stick to the grid system, despite the steep hills they cross.

Maybe it is the Painted Ladies, the old Victorian houses with their bright and multi-colored facades of rich ornamental stucco or exotically painted shingles and their extraordinary stained glass. Maybe it is the futuristic outlines of the modern skyscrapers, such as the pyramid of the Transamerica Building, or the dark and stern facade of the Bank of America.

Or maybe San Francisco's undeniable charm arises from the pairing of the old and the new, the past and the present, which can be found everywhere. Equally evident is the mood of her citizens. San Franciscans are great believers in street theater as is obvious from the number of singers, dancers and mimes that are to be found throughout the streets, the squares and the parks.

Most unforgettable is the extraordinary beauty of San Francisco at sunset, when the piers of the Golden Gate Bridge are dyed scarlet by the sun setting into a misty cloud. Then the city begins to turn on its lights, little by little, until the dark hills are outlined and illuminated by little pinpricks of light, including the strange and fabulous neon signs that amaze the passerby. At night San Francisco is still a most magical city.

44 One of the great views of San Francisco is that from the Golden Gate Bridge, surely one of the most romantic entrances to any major city in the world.

45 Even among the unusual skyscrapers of San Francisco, the pyramid of the Trans-america Building stands out. In the background can be seen the span of the Oakland Bay Bridge.

46-47 A panoramic view of San Francisco looking east toward Oakland. The grid system of the streets is clearly seen.

48 Since San Francisco is on a peninsula, the waterfront has always played an important role in the city's history.

49 The growth of San Francisco in the 1970s is responsible for the many new sky-scrapers in the commercial center of the city. In the background the Clock Tower on the Ferry Building can be easily seen.

50 The abundance of flowers is an essential part of San Francisco's charm, giving the city an air of eternal spring.

51 The World Headquarters Building of the Bank of America seen at sunset.

52-53 The many open-air performances by small theater groups or circuses are always assured of an enthusiastic audience.

54-55 Lombard Street winds down Russian Hill through banks of blooming hydrangeas.

56-57 The Painted Ladies are part of the unique charm of San Francisco. These Victorian houses, survivors of the fire of 1906, are built in four distinct styles: Queen Anne, Italianate, Stick and Georgian.

58 Since 1874, the cable cars have provided San Francisco with a unique form of public transport. Even the cable cars are Irish on St Patrick's Day.

59 Union Square, in the center of the city's elegant shopping area, is gaily decorated for St Patrick's Day.

60 In contrast to many American cities, the various ethnic groups in San Francisco seem to live together in harmony.

61 San Francisco's Chinatown, the largest Chinese community outside Asia, was established during the days of the Gold Rush.

62 The mixture of Chinese and Western cultures is evident throughout Chinatown.

63 It is not unusual to find street entertainers performing throughout the city's squares and parks.

64-65 Everywhere in San Francisco, there are places designed especially for children. Golden Gate Park has a vast playground set aside for their use.

66 The Golden Gate Bridge, designed by Joseph Strauss, was begun on 5 February 1933. The bridge was opened on 7 May 1937 by President Franklin Delano Roosevelt.

67 From a lookout point on the Marin County side of the bridge, one is aware of the extraordinary engineering techniques used to build the great piers.

68-69 The evening sky contrasts with the golden reflection of the sunset on San Francisco's skyline.

70 The Oakland Bay Bridge, opened in 1936, links San Francisco to the cities of Oakland and Berkeley.

71 A spectacular sunset bathes the hills of San Francisco in a golden glow.

72 top A magnificent view of the city can be seen from the Crown Room of the Fairmont Hotel.

72 bottom 'America' is one of the popular rock groups that frequently perform in San Francisco.

73 Even the seediest parts of the city seem exciting when ablaze with many — colored lights.

THE **C O N D O R**

BIG AL'S

ROARING 20's

NUDE GIRLS

CAROL DOD
TOPLESS

LOVE ACT

BIG AL'S

**TOTALLY NUDE
GIRLS ON STAG**

SEXSATIONAL

TOTALLY NUDE GIRL

NUDE

The Coast

The most obvious picture of the California coast is the well-known image of long white sand beaches crowded by young people, tanning in the sun or surfing over the powerful ocean waves. But early in the morning, these beaches reveal themselves in their own beauty, deserted, with all traces of human occupation erased from the sand overnight by the action of the ocean. The silence is interrupted only by the rhythmic sound of the waves and the haunting cries of the gulls and other sea birds. The growing warmth of the sun begins to dry the tangle of seaweed pushed up by the tide, while small crabs cautiously inspect the sandy shore for food. A change of light, and the silver reflections of the ocean dissolve to the wide spread of incredible blue as the sun climbs and the sea takes on the color of the sky above it. Later when the sun is blinding and hot, the crowds return, changing the beach once more.

North of San Diego, Long Beach and Santa Monica, running north toward San Francisco, lies the wild beauty of Big Sur. Here cliffs fall away to the sea, and the surrounding rocks look like nothing so much as a medieval fortress. The difficult access to the beach along tortuous paths has preserved the rugged beauty which is defined by the violence of the sea and the rocky shapes etched along the coast by wind, rain and time.

Just south of the Monterey Peninsula lies the Point Lobos State Reserve, one of the most evocative places on the coast of California. Here, in a protected area, live over 250 species of wild animals, from the squirrels and deer of the woodlands to the sea-lions and otters which frolic near the tide pools. It is also possible to see herds of whales and dolphins out at sea. The roarings of the sea lions, the crash of the waves, the cries of the seabirds, create a special atmosphere that even an influx of tourists can not spoil.

The hours of sunset are always the most beautiful along the water's edge. In the twilight the sounds of the woods and the sea are accentuated. The heat, which has been soaking into the rocks all day, slowly surrenders to the cold of night. When the light is gone, the shapes of the cliffs become hazy, indefinite, but the voice of the sea continues, deep and steady.

74 The coastline at Big Sur, though rocky and steep, is filled with blooming wild flowers in summer.

75 Smooth, sandy beaches can be found along the length of the Big Sur Highway.

76-77 A familiar landmark on the 17-mile drive between Carmel and Monterey is the Lone Cypress. A footpath follows the rocky shore below the famous tree.

78-79 The beach north of San Diego is especially wide, and the ocean waves are perfect for body surfing.

80-81 Water sports are very popular in California, where surfing is synonymous with
beach life.

82 Point Lobos State Reserve is a nature
preserve on the coast below Carmel. It is
known for the number of wild birds, otters and
sea lions that live along the shore.

83 The action of the Pacific Ocean at Morro
Bay has created strange natural sculptures on
the rocky shore.

84 The ebbing tide traces curious patterns in the sand of San Diego Beach.

85 *San Diego, close to the Mexican border, enjoys almost perfect weather, luring thousands of tourists to the beautiful beaches.*

86 The isolation of Big Sur is prized by many writers and artists.

87 Weather, among other natural causes, has modeled and carved the cliffs of Big Sur.

88 The beauty of the historic Mission San Carlos Borromeo del Rio Carmelo, in Carmel, founded in 1770, is set off by the perennial garden in the forecourt.

89 The famous Neptune pool is one of the highlights of a tour at San Simeon, the enormous house built by newspaper magnate William Randolph Hearst. Donated to the State, San Simeon contains priceless art treasures and rare objets d'art.

Deserts

Death Valley is one of the most famous deserts in the United States, covering a wide area with its alkali sand. Almost 20 percent of this territory is situated well below sea level, and Badwater, a salt water pool, is about 280 feet below sea level and the lowest point in the United States.

Long ago the Panamint Indians called this place 'Tomesha' — the land of fire. Death Valley's present name dates back to 1849, when a group of miners coming across from Nevada became lost in its inhospitable vastness and their adventure turned to tragedy. Today Death Valley has been declared a National Monument and is crossed by several well-marked roads where refreshments and accomodations can be found easily. Luckily the change created by human settlement has not spoiled the special beauty of this place.

Here nature created a series of amazing, almost lunar landscapes, everchanging as the constant wind moves the sand about, revealing the most incredible colors. One of the most extraordinary and variable parts of Death Valley is the Devil's Golf Course, where the border between reality and nightmare seems confused. Sand sculptures stand on a ghostly ground, as evening shadows move and lengthen.

The desert is a place where man feels his own impotence and inferiority, where it is most difficult to make nature submit to his will. In these desolate lands, on arid ground parched by the sun, it is only natural to muse on man's faults and mistakes. In the Mojave Desert, looking at the ruined ghost towns, with their memories of the curious period of the gold rush, this feeling increases. The dreams and hopes of easy wealth seem to be locked up in the burned clay of these hills, and on the dry slopes, changeless, but always different.

The same emotion is felt when looking at the Joshua Tree National Monument. The first pioneers crossing the desert were awestruck by the strange vegetation; and the huge yucca plants stretching to the sky reminded those weary men of the prophet Joshua raising his hands to the sky in prayer.

In fact, the desert reminds one again and again that nature is superior to man, asking the passerby eternally to respect what has been created by nature and inviting him to consider the future in the light of his past mistakes.

90 The great Ubehebe Crater in the heart of Death Valley was created by a volcanic eruption thousands of years ago.

91 The extraordinary shapes of Zabriskie Point in Death Valley are accentuated by the play of shadow and light.

92-93 Sunlight piercing the clouds above Zabriskie Point reveals the strange almost lunar landscape that is typical only of Death Valley.

94-95 Wind endlessly changes the desert landscape, moving the sand, exposing and then covering strange rock formations.

96-97 The unique landscape of Death Valley is the result of violent geological changes.

98 Like a kaleidescope, the patterns created by the wind in the sand dunes are ever-changing.

99 The contours of the dunes are a study of light and dark in the evening twilight.

100-101 The saline Badwater Pool at 280 feet below sea level in the lowest spot in Death Valley.

102 Despite the arid desert conditions, substantial vegetation survives here, having adapted to the extremes of temperature and climate.

103 The extraordinary desert flora includes over 600 species of plants which flower gloriously for a short time in the spring.

104 Dante's View in the Black Mountains is one of the most spectacular sights in this desolate region.

105 The Devil's Golf Course was created by the evaporation of a salt lake centuries ago which left an extraordinary surface of salt cystals upon the rugged surface.

106 The ruins of the Harmony Borax Works are the only remnant of the days in the nineteenth century when this land was mined for borax, which was carted by mule train across the desert.

107 In 1933, Death Valley was made a National Monument, and the small settlements expanded to cope with the tourist trade.

108-109 Palm Springs at the foot of San Jacinto Mountain is a well-known year-round resort.

110 Since 1930, Palm Springs has attracted numerous celebrities, some of whom have given their names to streets and roads.

111 Nicknamed the Winter Golf Capital of the World, Palm Springs has more than 40 courses within a 20-mile radius.

112-113 The Mojave Desert, which covers the high ground from the Colorado River in Nevada to the Sierra Nevada north of Los Angeles, is known for the curious types of cactus, including the yucca known as the Joshua Tree, which grow there.

Mountains

A large area of California is part of the imposing massif of the Sierra Nevada, whose rocky peaks rise to heights over 12,000 feet or more above the verdant Central Valley. Granite walls of an indescribable stateliness have been created by eons of erosion. Untouched valleys open among the mountains, and rivers wash down from the high slopes with an occasional cascading waterfall increasing the wild beauty of this area.

One of the most spectacular areas of the Sierra Nevada is Yosemite National Park. Established as a state park as long ago as 1864, it covers more than 1196 square miles. Named for the Indian tribe who lived there, Yosemite was created, like many other American parks, by John Muir, the indefatiguable naturalist who strenuously fought for the preservation of the American wilderness.

More than two and a half million tourists visit Yosemite every year, and it is miraculous that such a high number of visitors do not cause more damage to the natural environment. Very strict and severe regulations and unusual national pride are at the base of the American respect for nature. This may sound contradictory in view of the many cities and expanding industrialization to be found in California and the rest of the United States.

The change of the seasons deeply affects the aspects of the California Mountains. During the summer, the glare of the sun on the rocky peaks and granite walls is blinding, while in the valleys, the towering ancient sequoias and their wide spreading branches create pools of shadow. In winter a thick layer of snow covers the peaks and the waterfalls become amaxing ice sculptures. Once more, the parks are the uncontested realm of the wild animals.

114 The Sequoia National Park takes its name from the Sequoia sempervirens, the redwood which grows there that can reach a height over 300 feet.

115 Yosemite National Park contains three different landscapes: the valley, the giant sequoias, and an alpine wilderness threaded with fast-moving rivers.

116-117 The view from Sentinal Dome in Yosemite stretches away to the Sierra Nevada.

118-119 Yosemite is famous for the number of spectacular waterfalls found within the limits of the park.

120 Within the valleys in the Sierra Nevada can be found a number of small thriving ranches.

121 Yosemite Falls is the highest waterfall in the United States, over 1750 feet.

124 Yosemite, like the other national parks, has abundant wildlife. from tiny ground squirrels to the larger mammals such as deer and grizzly bear.

125 Rafting on the Merced River is a growing sport. The fishing there is a true test of skill, as it is a popular spot for trout, and well-fished.